THE MUMBAI
TRAVEL GUIDE

STEPHEN M HASTING

Map of Mumbai

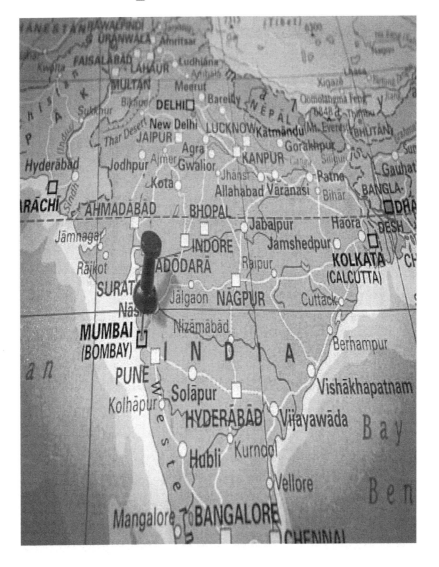

Table of contents

About the Book.

Welcome to the vibrant city of Mumbai, where tradition and modernity seamlessly blend to create a unique and captivating travel experience. This updated travel guide is your gateway to exploring the heart of India's financial capital, where bustling streets, historic landmarks, and a diverse cultural tapestry await your discovery.

Nestled along the Arabian Sea, Mumbai is a city that never sleeps, pulsating with energy day and night. From the iconic Gateway of India that stands as a symbol of the city's colonial past to the soaring skyscrapers of

Nariman Point that signify its rapid modernization, Mumbai presents an intriguing contrast of architectural marvels.

Indulge your taste buds in a culinary journey through its bustling markets and vibrant street food stalls, where you can savor local favorites like vada pav, pav bhaji, and bhel puri. For those seeking retail therapy, the city's bazaars and high-end malls offer a diverse range of shopping experiences, from traditional textiles and handicrafts to contemporary fashion brands. Immerse yourself in the city's rich cultural heritage by exploring its numerous museums, galleries, and historical sites. The Chhatrapati Shivaji Maharaj Terminus, a UNESCO World Heritage Site, is a stunning example of Victorian Gothic architecture that transports you back in time. Meanwhile, the Elephanta Caves on Elephanta Island provide a glimpse into ancient Indian art and spirituality.

Mumbai's entertainment scene is as diverse as its population. Catch a Bollywood movie screening at the iconic Regal Cinema or witness the fervor of a cricket match at the Wankhede Stadium. Take a leisurely stroll along the Marine Drive promenade, popularly known as the "Queen's Necklace," and watch the city lights dance on the waters of the Arabian Sea.

Whether you're exploring the historic neighborhoods of Colaba and Fort, experiencing the spirituality of Haji Ali Dargah, or simply soaking in the city's vivacious ambiance, Mumbai promises an unforgettable journey. This guide is designed to help you navigate through the city's myriad offerings, ensuring that you make the most of your time in this dynamic metropolis. Get ready to be enchanted by Mumbai's kaleidoscope of experiences!

Introduction.

The "Mumbai Travel Guide" is a comprehensive and captivating handbook that unveils the vibrant tapestry of India's bustling financial capital. Authored with meticulous attention to detail, this guide serves as an indispensable companion for both seasoned travelers and first-time explorers eager to immerse themselves in the city's myriad wonders.

Spanning over the pages of the book is a vivid exploration of Mumbai's unique blend of tradition and modernity. From the iconic Gateway of India that greets visitors with its historical significance to the towering skyscrapers that testify to the city's contemporary evolution, readers are taken on a visual journey that encapsulates Mumbai's architectural diversity.

The guide is a treasure trove of practical insights, offering readers a taste of the city's culinary delights through its bustling markets and street food stalls. The author's descriptions of local favorites like vada pav, pav bhaji, and bhel puri evoke the flavors of Mumbai's streets, inviting readers to embark on a gastronomic adventure.

With a keen eye for history and culture, the guide navigates through Mumbai's rich heritage, highlighting landmarks such as the Chhatrapati Shivaji Maharaj Terminus and the Elephanta Caves. These historical sites are presented as gateways to understanding the city's past, inviting readers to delve into the stories that have shaped Mumbai's identity.

Encompassing the vibrant entertainment scene, the guide captures the spirit of Mumbai's cinematic allure by mentioning the Regal Cinema and the thrill of cricket matches at the Wankhede Stadium. It also paints a vivid picture of the iconic Marine Drive, inviting readers to experience the poetic beauty of the "Queen's Necklace."

In essence, the "Mumbai Travel Guide" distills the essence of this cosmopolitan city into its pages, offering readers an invitation to explore its diverse neighborhoods, experience its spirituality, and revel in its dynamic ambiance. Seamlessly blending practical advice with cultural insights, this guide ensures that every traveler's journey through Mumbai is enriched and unforgettable.

Chapter 1: Introduction to Mumbai

Chapter 1 introduces Mumbai, a vibrant metropolis on India's west coast. Known as the financial capital, it blends history and modernity. With a rich cultural tapestry, Mumbai houses iconic landmarks like the Gateway of India and Marine Drive. The city's bustling local trains connect diverse neighborhoods, while Bollywood thrives as a global film hub. This chapter provides a glimpse into Mumbai's dynamic character, captivating millions with its energy and opportunities.

* Overview of Mumbai

Mumbai, a bustling coastal city in India, is renowned as the country's financial, cultural, and entertainment hub. Its rich history is reflected in landmarks like the Gateway of India, while modernity is evident in the towering skyscrapers of Nariman Point. The local train network is the lifeline of the city, connecting diverse neighborhoods. Home to Bollywood, the Hindi film industry, Mumbai also boasts vibrant street markets, like Colaba Causeway. Its unique blend of tradition and progress attracts millions, making Mumbai a captivating destination where dreams and ambitions converge amidst a lively, ever-evolving urban landscape.

* History of Mumbai

Mumbai's history is a tale of transformation and diversity. Originally a collection of fishing villages, it gained prominence when the Portuguese captured it in 1534. Later ceded to the British as part of the dowry of Catherine of Braganza, it grew as a major trading post. The 19th century saw Mumbai develop into a significant port under British rule, attracting migrants from different regions. The city played a pivotal role in India's struggle for independence, witnessing events like the Quit India Movement. In 1960, Maharashtra was formed with Mumbai as its capital. The city's growth continued, embracing global influences while retaining its local culture. Today, Mumbai stands as a dynamic metropolis, a testament to its resilient journey from humble origins to a cosmopolitan megacity.

* Culture and Diversity

Mumbai's culture is a vibrant mosaic, reflecting its diverse population. The city welcomes people from all over India and the world, creating a rich tapestry of traditions, languages, and cuisines. Festivals like Ganesh Chaturthi and Diwali unite its multi-religious populace in celebrations. The street food scene, from vada pav to pav bhaji, exemplifies its culinary diversity. Bollywood, deeply ingrained in the culture, transcends linguistic barriers. The city's cosmopolitan ethos fosters an environment where differences are celebrated, making

Mumbai a microcosm of India's unity in diversity.

Chapter 2: Planning Your Trip

Chapter 2 guides you in planning a memorable trip to Mumbai. Start by selecting the best time to visit, avoiding monsoons. Research accommodation options, ranging from luxury hotels to budget-friendly hostels. Learn about the city's transportation system, including the iconic local trains and taxis. Create an itinerary that covers must-see attractions like the Gateway of India, Elephanta Caves, and Marine Drive. Don't miss the bustling markets and street food stalls for an authentic experience. Familiarize yourself with local customs and safety tips. Whether you're a history buff, a foodie, or a culture enthusiast, Mumbai offers something unique for every traveler.

Best Time to Visit Mumbai

The best time to visit Mumbai is during the winter months, from November to February. This period offers comfortable temperatures and lower humidity levels, making it ideal for exploring the city's attractions. The monsoon season, from June to September, brings heavy rains that can disrupt outdoor plans. Summer, from March to May, is hot and humid, which might be challenging for some travelers. To enjoy pleasant weather and make the most of your trip, plan to visit Mumbai between November and February.

Duration of Stay

The ideal duration for a stay in Mumbai depends on your interests and itinerary. A short visit of 2 to 3 days can cover major attractions like the Gateway of India, Marine Drive, and Colaba Causeway. If you wish to explore the city's diverse culture, enjoy local cuisine, and experience the bustling markets, a stay of 4 to 5 days would be more fulfilling. This allows time for day trips to nearby attractions like Elephanta Caves as well. For a comprehensive experience, a week-long stay provides a balance between sightseeing, relaxation, and immersion in Mumbai's dynamic lifestyle.

* Visa Requirements

Travelers to Mumbai, India, need a valid visa to enter the country. Depending on your nationality and the purpose of your visit, you may apply for various types of visas, such as tourist, business, or e-visa. It's important to check with the Indian embassy or consulate in your country to understand the specific requirements, application process, and documentation needed for your visa category. Applying well in advance of your intended travel dates is recommended to ensure a smooth entry into Mumbai and to enjoy your trip without any hassles.

*Vaccinations and Health Tips

Before visiting Mumbai, ensure you're up-to-date on routine vaccines like measles, mumps, and rubella. Additionally, consider getting vaccines for hepatitis A and typhoid due to food and water concerns. Carry a small medical kit with basic medications, antiseptics, and any prescription drugs you need. Drink bottled water and avoid street food to minimize the risk of stomach issues. Protect yourself from mosquito-borne diseases by using repellent and wearing long sleeves. Be cautious in crowded areas to prevent illnesses. It's wise to have travel insurance covering medical emergencies. Consulting a healthcare professional before your trip is advised for personalized health recommendations.

* Currency and Exchange Rates

The currency used in Mumbai, India, is the Indian Rupee (INR). Exchange rates can vary, so it's recommended to check with reliable sources or currency exchange platforms before your trip. Currency exchange services are available at the airport, banks, and authorized exchange centers throughout the city. It's advisable to carry a mix of cash and credit/debit cards for convenience. Keep in mind that some smaller establishments might prefer cash transactions, so having local currency on hand can be helpful.

Chapter 3: Getting to Mumbai

Chapter 3 covers various ways of getting to Mumbai. The city is well-connected by air, with Chhatrapati Shivaji Maharaj International Airport serving as a major gateway. International and domestic flights offer convenience and accessibility. Mumbai is also connected by a vast railway network, making train travel a popular choice. Long-distance buses and road trips are viable options for those arriving from nearby cities. The chapter highlights the different modes of transportation, providing readers with insights into planning their journey to Mumbai, ensuring a smooth and enjoyable arrival experience.

* By Air

Traveling to Mumbai by air is convenient and efficient. Chhatrapati Shivaji Maharaj International Airport, one of India's busiest airports, serves both international and domestic flights. Major airlines connect Mumbai to various cities worldwide, making it accessible from different corners of the globe. The airport offers modern facilities, including lounges, dining options, and shopping outlets. Efficient transportation links connect the airport to the city center, ensuring a smooth transition upon arrival. Whether you're a global traveler or a domestic tourist, arriving in Mumbai by air provides a comfortable and well-connected entry point to the vibrant city.

* By Train

Traveling to Mumbai by train is a popular and immersive experience. The city boasts an extensive railway network, with several major train stations like Chhatrapati Shivaji Terminus (CST) and Mumbai Central. Trains offer various classes, from luxurious to budget-friendly, accommodating different preferences. Mumbai is well-connected to major cities across India via long-distance trains, providing travelers with a scenic journey and a glimpse into the diverse landscapes of the country. Train travel to Mumbai offers an authentic way to explore the region, interact with fellow passengers, and soak in the cultural tapestry that defines this bustling metropolis.

* By Road

Reaching Mumbai by road is possible through well-maintained highways and road networks. The city is connected to neighboring states and cities via a network of national and state highways. Long-distance buses operated by various companies offer affordable and convenient travel options, catering to different budgets. Additionally, road trips provide the flexibility to explore surrounding regions at your own pace. Mumbai's central location makes it accessible from multiple directions, allowing travelers to embark on scenic journeys and experience the changing landscapes as they approach the vibrant urban center.

Chapter 4: Accommodation Options

Chapter 4 outlines diverse accommodation options in Mumbai. The city offers a range of choices to suit different budgets and preferences. Luxury hotels such as The Taj Mahal Palace provide opulent experiences, while boutique hotels offer unique charm. Business travelers can find comfort in upscale accommodations like Trident Nariman Point. Budget-friendly hostels cater to backpackers and solo travelers. Airbnb and serviced apartments offer homely stays for extended visits. Whether you seek lavish comfort or a budget-friendly stay, this chapter provides insights into selecting the perfect accommodation to enhance your Mumbai experience.

*Luxury Hotels

Mumbai boasts an array of luxury hotels that promise opulent experiences. The iconic Taj Mahal Palace, overlooking the Arabian Sea, exudes old-world charm and modern luxury. The Oberoi Mumbai impresses with its impeccable service and stunning city views. Trident Nariman Point combines business amenities with elegance. The St. Regis Mumbai offers lavish rooms and a vibrant nightlife scene. These establishments offer world-class facilities, gourmet dining, spa treatments, and more. Catering to discerning travelers, Mumbai's luxury hotels ensure a sophisticated and indulgent stay, complementing the city's vibrant ambiance with a touch of refined comfort.

* Mid-range Hotels

For travelers seeking a comfortable stay without breaking the bank, Mumbai offers an array of mid-range hotels. Hotel Residency Fort provides a central location and modern amenities. The Mirador offers a blend of convenience and value near the airport. The Regale by Tunga combines modern comfort with personalized service. These mid-range options cater to business and leisure travelers, offering comfortable rooms, essential facilities, and convenient locations. With affordable rates and quality services, these hotels ensure a pleasant stay that balances comfort and cost, making them ideal choices for those looking for a balance between luxury and budget.

* Budget Hotels

Mumbai accommodates budget-conscious travelers with a selection of budget hotels. Hotel Godwin offers a central location and straightforward amenities. Hotel Accord provides comfortable rooms at affordable rates. Backpacker Panda Colaba welcomes budget travelers with a social atmosphere. These options focus on practicality, offering clean rooms, basic facilities, and often communal spaces for interaction. Ideal for those who prioritize exploration over luxury, these budget hotels allow you to experience Mumbai without straining your wallet. With convenient locations and wallet-friendly rates, these accommodations are a great choice for travelers seeking affordability without compromising on a memorable Mumbai experience.

Chapter 5: Exploring Mumbai Neighborhoods

Chapter 5 delves into Mumbai's diverse neighborhoods, each offering unique experiences. South Mumbai boasts historic sites like the Gateway of India and Colaba Causeway's bustling markets. Bandra's hip vibe features trendy cafes and shopping. Juhu and Versova offer beachfront charm and lively nightlife. Dadar's cultural hub showcases local art and traditional eateries. Further, Powai's modernity contrasts with the historic Elephanta Island. Whether you seek history, culture, entertainment, or relaxation, this chapter guides you through the distinct neighborhoods of Mumbai, helping you navigate the city's various facets and discover the essence of each vibrant enclave.

* South Mumbai

South Mumbai, often referred to as "SoBo," is the historical heart of the city. It boasts iconic landmarks like the Gateway of India, Chhatrapati Shivaji Terminus (CST), and the heritage precinct of Colaba Causeway. The area's colonial-era architecture and vibrant street life create a unique atmosphere. Marine Drive offers a picturesque promenade along the Arabian Sea, while Nariman Point stands as a business and commercial hub. Art galleries, museums, and charming cafes add to the area's cultural richness. South Mumbai encapsulates Mumbai's colonial past, bustling markets, and a blend of old-world charm and modern vibrancy.

* Bandra

Bandra, a trendy neighborhood, embodies Mumbai's contemporary culture. Known as the "Queen of Suburbs," it's a fusion of old-world charm and modern energy. The Bandra-Worli Sea Link connects it to South Mumbai. This area is a hub of creative spaces, fashion boutiques, and diverse dining options. The iconic Bandra Fort offers stunning sea views. Bandstand Promenade attracts locals and visitors alike, while Mount Mary Church adds a touch of spirituality. With its artistic flair, upscale boutiques, and lively nightlife, Bandra reflects Mumbai's cosmopolitan character, making it a must-visit for those seeking a vibrant urban experience.

* Juhu and Andheri

Juhu and Andheri, bustling suburbs in Mumbai's western region, offer a blend of leisure and urban charm. Juhu Beach is a popular hangout spot, known for its iconic sunset views and street food stalls. The area's lively atmosphere is matched by the vibrant Versova Beach. Andheri, a thriving commercial hub, houses Bollywood studios and trendy cafes. Lokhandwala Market attracts shoppers, while the nightlife along Link Road is vibrant. Both neighborhoods showcase Mumbai's modernity, with a mix of entertainment, beachfront relaxation, and urban lifestyle, making them magnets for residents and visitors seeking diverse experiences.

Chapter 6: Top Attractions in Mumbai

Chapter 6 highlights Mumbai's top attractions. The Gateway of India stands as an iconic landmark, while Chhatrapati Shivaji Terminus boasts architectural grandeur. Marine Drive offers a captivating promenade, and Elephanta Caves showcase ancient rock-cut temples. Juhu Beach's vibrant atmosphere and Haji Ali Dargah's spiritual aura add diversity. The bustling markets of Colaba Causeway and Crawford Market are shopper's paradises. Mumbai's film world comes alive at Bollywood Studios. Art enthusiasts can explore the Chhatrapati Shivaji Maharaj Vastu Sangrahalaya and Jehangir Art Gallery. This chapter guides readers through the city's must-visit sites, offering a glimpse into Mumbai's rich heritage, culture, and modernity.

* Gateway of India

The Gateway of India, Mumbai's iconic landmark, stands proudly overlooking the Arabian Sea. Built during the British colonial era, it welcomes visitors with its Indo-Saracenic architecture and intricate details. The arch stands as a symbol of historical significance, witnessing the city's past and present. Tourists gather here to marvel at the sea breeze and take boat rides to Elephanta Island. The Gateway also holds cultural events, serving as a gathering place for celebrations and protests alike. Its prominent location and historical resonance make it an essential stop for anyone exploring Mumbai's heritage and coastal beauty.

Elephanta Caves

The Elephanta Caves, a UNESCO World Heritage Site, feature ancient rock-cut temples on Elephanta Island. Accessible by boat from Mumbai, these intricate cave carvings depict Hindu deities and mythological stories. A captivating journey into India's history and spirituality, the caves offer a unique experience just a short distance from Mumbai's bustling shores.

Juhu Beach

Juhu Beach, a bustling coastal stretch in Mumbai's western suburbs, offers a blend of leisure and energy. Known for its lively atmosphere and stunning sunsets, it's a popular spot for locals and tourists alike. The beachfront is adorned with food stalls offering Mumbai's street delicacies, while activities like horse rides and beach volleyball create a vibrant ambiance. Juhu's iconic skyline hosts luxurious hotels and celebrities' residences. The Versova Beach extension adds to the charm. Whether you're looking for a relaxed stroll, a taste of Mumbai's street food, or a glimpse into local life, Juhu Beach offers a captivating experience.

* Bollywood Film City

Mumbai's Bollywood Film City is a captivating destination for film enthusiasts. This sprawling complex houses studios, sets, and production facilities where India's iconic films are made. Guided tours offer insights into the filmmaking process, celebrity encounters, and a chance to witness the magic behind one of the world's largest film industries.

Chapter 7: Local Cuisine and Dining

Chapter 7 explores Mumbai's diverse culinary scene. From street food to fine dining, the city offers a gastronomic adventure. Try iconic dishes like vada pav and pav bhaji, savor coastal flavors with seafood at Juhu, and explore Parsi delicacies in Dadar. Chowpatty Beach's stalls offer delectable chaats, while Mohammed Ali Road's Ramadan feast delights foodies.

Trendy Bandra houses eclectic cafes, while Colaba's restaurants serve global cuisines. Irani cafes and South Indian eateries showcase Mumbai's cultural fusion. Whether you're a food connoisseur or a casual diner, this chapter guides you through a culinary journey that captures the essence of Mumbai's flavors.

* Introduction to Mumbai's Cuisine

Mumbai's cuisine is a vibrant tapestry woven from diverse culinary traditions. Influenced by its multicultural population and coastal location, the city's food scene is a melting pot of flavors. Street food is a highlight, with iconic dishes like vada pav (spicy potato fritter in a bun) and pav bhaji (vegetable curry served with buttered bread). Coastal delights include succulent seafood and spicy Konkani dishes. Irani cafes offer nostalgia with their bun maska and chai. From Parsi delicacies to global fusion, Mumbai's food culture reflects its cosmopolitan identity, making it a paradise for those seeking diverse and delectable culinary experiences.

* Popular Local Restaurants

Mumbai is home to a plethora of popular local restaurants that offer a wide range of flavors. Britannia & Co. in Ballard Estate serves Parsi delights, while Trishna near Fort is known for its coastal seafood. Bademiya in Colaba offers scrumptious kebabs, and Café Leopold is an iconic spot for international fare. Gajalee specializes in Malvani seafood, while Prakash Upahaar Kendra serves South Indian treats. Indigo

Delicatessen in Colaba and The Table in Colaba and Bandra offer contemporary global cuisines. These eateries are an integral part of Mumbai's culinary landscape, offering a taste of both local traditions and modern culinary creativity.

Chapter 8: Outdoor Activities and Day Trips

Chapter 8 guides you through outdoor activities and day trips around Mumbai. Embrace the sea breeze at Marine Drive or visit Sanjay Gandhi National Park for nature trails. Explore Elephanta Island's ancient caves or escape to the hill station of Matheran. Lonavala's lush landscapes and Karjat's adventure sports provide thrilling getaways. Alibaug's beaches offer relaxation, while Elephanta Festival and Kala Ghoda Arts Festival celebrate culture. Enjoy the tranquility of Global Vipassana Pagoda or the spirituality of Haji Ali Dargah. This chapter unveils a variety of outdoor pursuits and day-trip options, allowing you to experience Mumbai's surroundings beyond its urban confines.

* Sanjay Gandhi National Park

Sanjay Gandhi National Park, nestled within Mumbai's urban sprawl, is a verdant oasis. It offers a diverse range of outdoor activities and natural beauty. The park features dense forests, scenic walking trails, and ancient Buddhist caves at Kanheri. It's home to various wildlife species, including leopards and deer. The park's tranquil environment provides an escape from the city's hustle and bustle, making it a popular spot for picnics, nature walks, and birdwatching. Whether you seek serenity, a glimpse of history, or a connection with nature, Sanjay Gandhi National Park offers a rejuvenating experience within Mumbai's boundaries.

* Elephanta Island

Elephanta Island, a short boat ride from Mumbai, houses the UNESCO-listed Elephanta Caves. These ancient rock-cut temples showcase intricate sculptures depicting Hindu deities and mythological stories. The main Shiva temple, with its imposing Trimurti sculpture, is a centerpiece. The island's lush surroundings add to the allure. The journey to Elephanta offers serene sea views, while the caves provide a unique blend of spirituality and history. This day trip from Mumbai allows you to step into a world of ancient artistry and mythology, providing a captivating glimpse into India's cultural heritage.

Chapter 9: Cultural Experiences

Chapter 9 delves into Mumbai's cultural tapestry, offering immersive experiences. Visit Chhatrapati Shivaji Maharaj Terminus to admire its architectural grandeur. The Chhatrapati Shivaji Maharaj Vastu Sangrahalaya and Jehangir Art Gallery showcase art and history. Dhobi Ghat, the world's largest open-air laundry, provides a unique insight into local life. Witness the dabbawalas' efficient lunch delivery system. Participate in the Ganesh Chaturthi festival, and explore Mahalaxmi Dhobi Ghat's traditional laundry practices. The chapter invites you to engage with Mumbai's heritage, traditions, and daily life, offering a deeper understanding of the city's vibrant culture and diverse communities.

* Festivals and Celebrations

Mumbai's festivals and celebrations reflect its rich cultural diversity. Ganesh Chaturthi, a grand spectacle, honors Lord Ganesha with elaborate processions and vibrant decorations. Diwali illuminates the city with lights and fireworks. Navaratri sees energetic dance performances during the nine-night celebration. Eid, Christmas, and Holi bring communities together in festive spirit. The Kala Ghoda Arts Festival showcases Mumbai's creativity, while the Elephanta Festival features music and dance on the island. These festivities not only celebrate religious and cultural traditions but also offer a chance to immerse yourself in the city's joyful atmosphere and witness its harmonious coexistence of various communities

* Traditional Crafts and Markets

Mumbai's traditional crafts and markets are a treasure trove of local artistry. Colaba Causeway and Linking Road offer a range of clothing, accessories, and souvenirs. Crawford Market presents a colorful array of fruits, spices, and flowers. Dharavi's bustling markets showcase leather goods, pottery, and textiles. Chor Bazaar is a haven for antiques and vintage finds. Kala Ghoda Arts Precinct features boutiques and galleries. Exploring these markets unveils Mumbai's creative pulse and local craftsmanship, providing opportunities to take home unique mementos and gain insight into the city's commerce, creativity, and centuries-old trading heritage.

* Religious and Spiritual Sites

Mumbai embraces diverse religious and spiritual sites. Siddhivinayak Temple, dedicated to Lord Ganesha, attracts devotees. Haji Ali Dargah, a mosque off the coast, offers a serene experience. Mahalaxmi Temple honors the goddess of wealth. The Global Vipassana Pagoda stands as a symbol of peace and tranquility. Mount Mary Church in Bandra is a Christian pilgrimage spot. The Jewish Synagogue in Byculla represents Mumbai's Jewish heritage. These sites exemplify Mumbai's religious harmony, offering a glimpse into its varied faiths and providing spaces for reflection, devotion, and cultural exploration amidst the city's dynamic landscape.

* Heritage Walks and Tours

Embark on heritage walks and tours to uncover Mumbai's history. The Ballard Estate walk reveals colonial-era architecture. The Fort Heritage District showcases historical landmarks like Rajabai Clock Tower. Dharavi tours offer insights into local industry and community. The Art Deco walk in Marine Drive unveils architectural gems. Explore Elephanta Island's ancient caves with guided tours. Discover the city's culinary heritage through food walks in iconic neighborhoods. These immersive experiences allow you to step back in time, explore hidden corners, and understand Mumbai's evolution, providing a deeper connection to its past and present.

Chapter 10: Practical Information

Chapter 10 provides essential practical information for navigating Mumbai. It covers transportation, including the local train network and taxis, guiding you on fares and routes. It outlines safety tips for avoiding tourist scams and staying aware in crowded areas. The chapter offers insights into local customs and etiquette, helping you navigate cultural nuances respectfully. Currency exchange options, emergency contact numbers, and healthcare facilities are also highlighted. With guidance on communication, weather, and adapting to Mumbai's dynamic lifestyle, this chapter equips you with the necessary tools to navigate the city smoothly and enjoy a fulfilling visit.

* Safety Tips

Ensure a safe visit to Mumbai with these tips. Keep your belongings secure in crowded areas and be cautious with personal items. Use reputable transportation services and negotiate fares before boarding. Avoid walking alone in poorly lit areas at night. Be cautious of overly friendly strangers offering assistance. Use reliable sources for currency exchange and carry a mix of cash and cards. Respect local customs and dress codes when visiting religious sites. Stay hydrated and protect yourself from the sun. Keep emergency numbers and your accommodation's contact details handy. Staying aware and practicing common-sense precautions will help you enjoy a worry-free experience in Mumbai.

*Useful Phrases

Master these useful phrases to navigate Mumbai with ease. "Namaste" for greetings, "Kripya" for requesting assistance, "Kitna hua?" to ask for prices, "Kahan hai?" for asking directions, and "Khana kahaan milega?" to inquire about food locations. Say "Dhanyavaad" for thank you and "Shukriya" for expressing gratitude. When bargaining, use "Thoda kam ho sakta hai?" to negotiate. "Mujhe English nahi aati" means "I don't know English." "Mujhe yahaan le chalo" is "Take me here." These phrases will enhance your interactions, make navigating the city smoother, and foster a warm connection with locals during your Mumbai journey.

Communication

*Emergency Services

Communication in Mumbai is predominantly in Hindi and English. Most locals understand basic English, making communication with taxi drivers, vendors, and locals easier. Learning a few Hindi phrases can enhance interactions. For emergencies, dial 100 for police assistance, 101 for fire emergencies, and 102 for medical help. Keep your accommodation's address and phone number handy, and consider having a local SIM card for convenient communication. Many areas offer free Wi-Fi, enabling easy access to online maps and communication apps. Staying connected and informed enhances your safety and experience in Mumbai.

* Conclusion

In conclusion, exploring Mumbai is an exhilarating journey through history, culture, and modernity. From the iconic Gateway of India to the bustling streets of Colaba Causeway, this city embraces diversity and offers something for every traveler. Mumbai's vibrant neighborhoods, rich culinary scene, and cultural landmarks create an immersive experience. As you navigate the local customs, indulge in street food, and visit historical sites, you'll uncover the layers of this dynamic metropolis. Whether you're drawn to its bustling markets, serene beaches, or architectural marvels, Mumbai's unique blend of tradition and progress ensures an unforgettable adventure that captures the essence of India's captivating urban spirit.

Printed in Great Britain
by Amazon

28045977R00035